ISBN: 1-884850-03-0   FIRST EDITION

Library of Congress Catalog Card Number: 94-66531

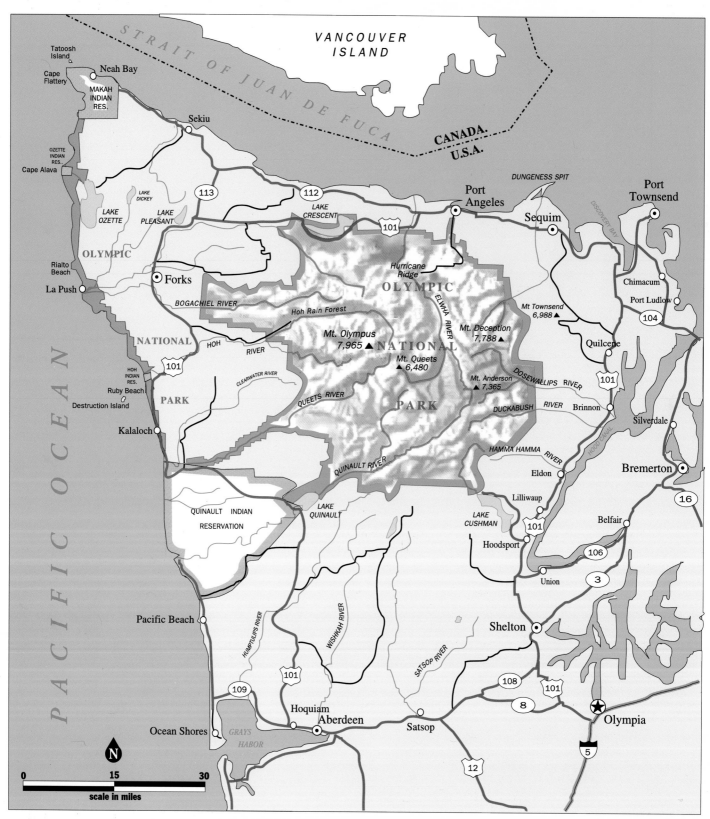

VANCOUVER ISLAND

STRAIT OF JUAN DE FUCA

CANADA.
U.S.A.

Tatoosh Island
Neah Bay
Cape Flattery
MAKAH INDIAN RES.

Sekiu

OZETTE INDIAN RES..
Cape Alava

LAKE DICKEY
LAKE OZETTE
LAKE PLEASANT

113
112

LAKE CRESCENT

DUNGENESS SPIT

Port Angeles

Sequim

Port Townsend

DISCOVERY BAY

101

OLYMPIC

Hurricane Ridge

OLYMPIC

Chimacum
Port Ludlow

104

Rialto Beach
Forks

La Push

BOGACHIEL RIVER

Hoh Rain Forest

Mt Townsend 6,988 ▲

Mt. Olympus 7,965 ▲

ELWHA RIVER

Mt. Deception 7,788 ▲

Quilcene

NATIONAL

HOH

RIVER

Mt. Queets ▲ 6,480

NATIONAL

101

HOH INDIAN RES.
Ruby Beach
Destruction Island

CLEARWATER RIVER

Mt. Anderson ▲ 7,365

DOSEWALLIPS RIVER

101

Silverdale

PARK

QUEETS RIVER

PARK

DUCKABUSH RIVER

Brinnon

Kalaloch

QUINAULT RIVER

HAMMA HAMMA RIVER

Bremerton

LAKE QUINAULT

Eldon

16

QUINAULT INDIAN RESERVATION

Lilliwaup

LAKE CUSHMAN

Belfair

101

106

Hoodsport

3

Union

Pacific Beach

HUMPTULIPS RIVER

WISHKAH RIVER

SATSOP RIVER

Shelton

101

108

101

8

109

101

Olympia

Hoquiam
Aberdeen

Satsop

Ocean Shores

GRAYS HABOR

5

12

N

0   15   30

scale in miles

PACIFIC OCEAN

GALE ENGELKE

2

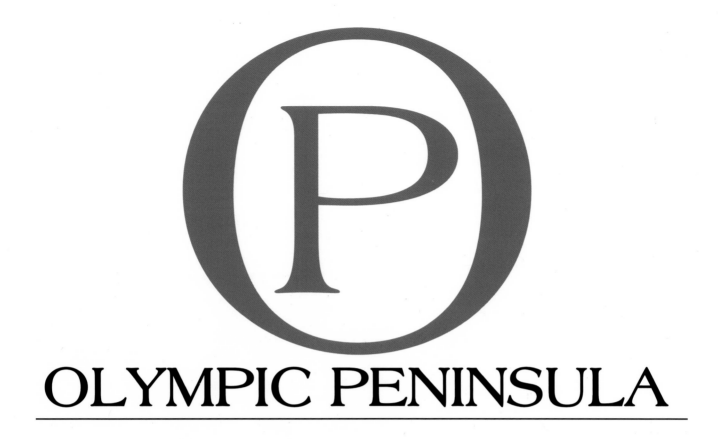

OLYMPIC PENINSULA

PHOTOGRAPHED BY

PATRICK TEHAN
LYNN SAUNDERS
LARRY STEAGALL
STEVE ZUGSCHWERDT

TEXT BY

SEABURY BLAIR JR.

THE SUN

Edited & Designed By
J. BRUCE BAUMANN

Listen now to the raven
OLYMPIC PENINSULA

YOU are standing on the summit of the Olympic Peninsula, 7,965 feet above sea level. Glaciers five miles long and 30 stories deep spiral outward from Mount Olympus. The ice embraces this mountain like the snowy Olympic ridges all around you. The ridges roll and twist in a widening oval to the western edge of the continent. A black Olympic Raven wheels on air currents above you, croaking. Tribes of the Peninsula give this bird magical god-like powers.

You can look across an area of more than 4,600 square miles from here; from the emerald stretch of Hood Canal to the east to that ruby haze in the west where the Pacific Ocean gobbles the sky. To the south, ridges turn from red to purple as they retreat from the summer dawn. To the north, a rugged jumble of mountains tumbles toward the Strait of Juan de Fuca.

You gain a rare perspective from here on this summit, near the geographic center of the Olympic Peninsula. Many of the major rivers gnawing at these mountains are born of the glaciers at your feet. You likely slogged 16 miles along the Hoh River Trail to begin your

Hood Canal, a 50-mile-long fjord carved by a continental glacier, is the saltwater link between the Olympic and Kitsap Peninsulas.

A rare harlequin duck takes wing on the Dosewallips River. Viewing wildlife is a popular Peninsula activity.

the national park surrounding you as you stand at the summit of Mount Olympus — people come simply to look in wonder at these woods, these mountains, this primeval glacial ice. There are easily loftier peaks than the Olympics, larger trees in other forests, more rugged rivers, longer glaciers, broader beaches. But nowhere in the Lower 48 and pitifully few other places on the North American continent can you find them within a long day's walk of each other. Such natural diversity is what makes this place so attractive.

Not all of the rivers on the Peninsula sprout from glaciers of Mount Olympus. But stand on its summit and follow the raven around to the rising sun. Look southeast until you see the mountain with the glacier Olympic trail guide author Robert L. Wood once described as "a big ghost." It is Mount Queets, and the left arm of the ghost points to Dodwell-Rixon Pass. There is the birthplace of the Elwha River.

Theodore Rixon and Arthur Dodwell were U.S. Geological Survey workers who spent three years at the turn of the century mapping the Olympic Peninsula. They charted more than 3,400 square miles by 1900, only 16 of which had been logged. The pass named for them leads to the Elwha Snowfinger, at the heart of the Olympic backcountry.

You can backpack near the bottom of the snowfinger on

You can always fly a kite at Ocean Shores, on the southwestern tip of the Peninsula. The resort area is also one of the few places where you can drive a vehicle on the beach.

excellent trail. Drive to the end of the Elwha River Road at Whiskey Bend. From here, trek 34 miles up the river and at trail's end, ford the infant river. Climb through brush and meadow about two miles, and look down to the spot where the Elwha bubbles from underneath the snow.

Snowmelt fathers the Elwha, not glacial ice. Though the river carries tons of soil on its northerly journey to the Strait of Juan de Fuca, it carries none of the flour ground by glacier. Because it rattles toward the Strait to the east of your perch on Olympus, it passes through a drier part of the Peninsula. Olympus catches clouds sweeping off the Pacific and wrings the rain from them. Here, where you stand, more than 240 inches of rain falls every year. There, at the spot where the Elwha is born, perhaps half that amount of precipitation falls. Thirty miles downstream, it rains less than 25 inches per year.

Folks celebrate the "Rain Shadow" in Sequim's annual Irrigation Festival. Only 17 inches of rain falls on Sequim every year. If it is raining most places on the Peninsula and you want sunshine, visit Sequim or the nearby Dungeness Spit.

The Elwha River was one of the first to be visited by white men when in 1889, James H. Christie led a band of adventurers on the first trans-

Kelp fronds wash up on rocks at Tongue Point on the Strait of Juan de Fuca. The sea plant attaches to rock anchors and has a bulb-like float to keep the fronds near surface sunlight.

One of the tastiest morsels served up by the waters around the Peninsula is the Hood Canal shrimp. Traditionally sought during the last two weeks of May, the canal spot shrimp are larger than their cousins elsewhere around the Peninsula. Washington Department of Fisheries and Wildlife licenses are required; available anywhere in the state. Best bait for the traps, or shrimp pots? Puss N' Boots Cat Food. Ask anyone.

Hood Canal curves like a 50-mile hook around the Olympic Peninsula to the west and the Kitsap Peninsula to the east. The Olympic Mountains form a barrier to storms sweeping from the Pacific Ocean.

STEVE ZUGSCHWERDT

LYNN SAUNDERS

38

LYNN SAUNDERS

LYNN SAUNDERS

Coho salmon — smaller than the big chinooks or kings — begin their life cycle in a hatchery near Hoodsport, at the southeastern corner of the Peninsula. Tim Ward and Drew Burkhard, left, work the fish ready to spawn. Forty days later, 8,000 coho are almost ready to hatch. Dark spots in the eggs are the eyes of the fish. At 75 days, the baby coho are called fry. Coho are the most seriously depleted of the types of salmon found on the Peninsula, which include the chinook and chum.

STEVE ZUGSCHWERDT

STEVE ZUGSCHWERDT

Janalynn Melseth, who lives on the eastern shore of the Peninsula in Quilcene, is training her goats to be pack animals. She says they are more sure-footed than other pack animals, which may be important in the high Olympic country.

51

Most of the people who work in the forest are called loggers, although many don't cut down trees. Tom Trent, a Quilcene forest worker, rigs a choker cable 30 feet up the trunk of a fir tree to be used as a yarding tower. The cable will drag logs to a staging area, where other "loggers" will load them on to a truck and drive them to a scaling station. Here, folks like Tom Keglie of Poulsbo will measure the diameter of each cut log and enter the measurements on a hand-held computer.

Rafts of logs are a common sight around the Peninsula. Bays and inlets are collecting points for the logs, which are stored to be towed to the mills in communities like Port Gamble, Port Angeles, Aberdeen or Shelton.

PATRICK TEHAN

California sea lions, once endangered, are considered something of an overpopulated nuisance around parts of the Peninsula. The animals compete with other predators, anglers and commercial fishers for disappearing runs of salmon.

LYNN SAUNDERS

STEVE ZUGSCHWERDT

Victorian houses built in the second half of the 19th Century have been restored and are homes to some of the workers in the old company town of Port Gamble. The homes are still the property of the logging firm, Pope and Talbot Inc. The milltown is on the northern tip of the Kitsap Peninsula and is a popular spot for weekend outings.

The Port Gamble Cemetery includes gravestones more than a century old — which is ancient for this relatively new country. White man first crossed the Olympic Peninsula in 1889 and 1890, although towns around the coast are older. One gravestone in the cemetery tells the story of a pioneer who lost his head during a battle with the Indians.

LARRY STEAGALL

Port Townsend, on the northeastern tip of the Olympic Peninsula, celebrates its maritime heritage with a Wooden Boat Festival every September. Old schooners and square-riggers stage a race and folks like chocolatier Cliff Perry serve up sweets. September is also one of the months the city hosts a tour of its restored Victorian homes. The homes are also open for tours in May.

LARRY STEAGALL

LARRY STEAGALL

Typical of the restored architecture of Port Townsend is the Starrett House, built in 1889 and now a splendid bed and breakfast. Owners Edel and Bob Sokol are likely to welcome guests from the free-hung, three-tiered spiral staircase. In May, Chetzemoka Park in the city overflows with flowers and the community celebrates the blooming of wild rhododendron, which turn most of the Olympic Peninsula pink with their blossoms.

LARRY STEAGALL

LARRY STEAGALL

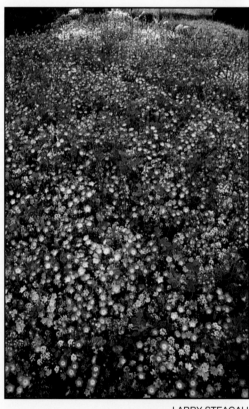

LARRY STEAGALL

Fort Worden State Park is the site of an annual summer jazz and fine arts festival, writing and arts seminars and a kayaking symposium in the autumn. Family reunions often are held in some of the quarters of the old fort, abandoned after World War II. Residents can rent some of the quarters by contacting the state park. The park, and a downtown motel, were also the on-location sites for the filming of the movie, "An Officer and a Gentleman."

STEVE ZUGSCHWERDT

PATRICK TEHAN (ABOVE AND LEFT)

Water is everywhere on the Olympic Peninsula. Creeks chatter through the rain forest to feed rivers like the Sol Duc, while next to the river, visitors play in hot springs thought to originate from the same source as those at Olympic Hot Springs. Sol Duc Hot Springs Resort is open from Memorial Day to Labor Day. Thousands stay at an auto campground across the river and hike trails nearby.

Forests in the winter Olympics seem to stretch endlessly.

LYNN SAUNDERS

LYNN SAUNDERS

Cape Flattery at Neah Bay is the northwestern-most point in the Lower 48, where the Pacific Ocean pours into the Strait of Juan de Fuca. Just east of Cape Flattery is Neah Bay, the home of the Makah Tribe. These Native Americans were renowned whalers. A museum in Neah Bay is open year-round.

PATRICK TEHAN

STEVE ZUGSCHWERDT

STEVE ZUGSCHWERDT

Olympus Guard Station is in the rain forest, nine miles and halfway up the Hoh River Trail between the glacial birthplace of the river on Mount Olympus and the end of the road. A three-sided shelter keeps hikers dry in frequent rains and Olympic National Park rangers staff the station in the summer. Hikers often find the moss-covered roots of trees good resting spots. Many of the mosses draping the trees in the rain forest are called ephiphytes, or air-breathers. They have no roots and don't harm the trees.

STEVE ZUGSCHWERDT

Just past Olympus Guard Station, hikers can turn left at a trail junction and climb more than 4,000 feet in six miles to the Olympic alpine country of Seven Lakes Basin. Gone are the giant trees of the rain forest, replaced by silver fir and mountain hemlock groomed by the wind and snow. Seven Lakes Basin, which actually has more than a dozen lakes, is a popular backpacking destination.

Daffodils grow in the shadow of the Satsop nuclear power plant along the southern edge of the Peninsula. Stacks from the abandoned WPPS nuclear project are nearby. Many of the flowers are sold or used in Tacoma's Daffodil Festival every spring. The Grays Harbor County Courthouse in Montesano shows off a unique domed ceiling.

Residents of Bremerton can look across the Kitsap Peninsula to the waters of Hood Canal and the Olympic Mountains to the west. The Brothers, Mount Jupiter and Mount Constance, from left, are the peaks which appear highest from this vantage point. The city is the home of Puget Sound Naval Shipyard, where early nuclear attack submarines are being cut up for scrap.

STEVE ZUGSCHWERDT

Water links the Kitsap and Olympic Peninsulas. To the north, the Foulweather Bluff Nature Conservancy looks across to the Olympic Mountains. Wetlands support wildlife to the south.